This book is a companion volume to *The Wild Romancer – Uncovering the Romance Jesus Longs to Lavish on You*. While this volume can easily stand alone, you will find that you get much more out of it by using it alongside *The Wild Romancer*.

To learn more about Brenda's ministry visit:

www.brendacobbmurphy.com

The WILD ROMANCER Journey Guide

THE WILD ROMANCER JOURNEY GUIDE

Your Personal Journey into Intimacy with Jesus

BRENDA COBB MURPHY

The Wild Romancer Journey Guide
Your Personal Journey into Intimacy with Jesus
All rights reserved.
Copyright © 2010 Brenda Cobb Murphy
V2.0

This book may not be reproduced, transmitted, or stored in whole or in part by any means, including graphic, electronic, or mechanical without the express written consent of the publisher except in the case of brief quotations embodied in critical articles and reviews.

We prefer to call Holy Spirit by His name, instead of talking *about* Him by adding "the" in front of His name.

The name satan and related names are not capitalized. We like the way Destiny Image Publishers put it, "We choose not to acknowledge him, even to the point of violating grammatical rules."

Unless otherwise indicated, all Scriptural quotations are from the *New International Version* (NIV) of the Bible. Copyright © 1973, 1978, 1984 by International Bible Society.
Scripture quotations noted AMP are from The Amplified Bible: New Testament.
Scripture quotations noted KJV are from The King James Version of the Bible.

Cover photo by Zeljko Radojko/Shutterstock.com
Cover design by Brenda Cobb Murphy but it exists because of Micah Lee

ISBN: 978-1490438641

ISBN: 1490438645

PRINTED IN THE UNITED STATES OF AMERICA

To all of you who asked "But when are you going to write the book telling how I can have this relationship myself?"

And to

Jan Clark, who endured, encouraged, and carried me as I whined, cried, and complained my way through the ordeal of getting this done. You are an amazing BFF!

TABLE OF CONTENTS

YOUR JOURNEY GUIDE   1

WHAT TO PACK   3

BEGINNING THE JOURNEY   5

HE'S DESPERATE FOR YOUR LOVE   7

WHAT TO EXPECT   11

SOME THINGS THAT MIGHT HELP   15

OTHER HELPRUL HINTS   19

IS THIS JOURNEY SAFE?   23

USE YOUR NOTEBOOK!   29

EXERCISES   31

CHAPTER ONE   33

CHAPTER TWO   41

CHAPTER THREE   45

CHAPTER FOUR   51

CHAPTER FIVE   57

CHAPTER SIX   63

CHAPTER SEVEN   69

CHAPTER EIGHT   73

CHAPTER NINE   77

CHAPTER TEN   81

CHAPTER ELEVEN   85

CHAPTER TWELVE   89

CONTINUING THE JOURNEY   93

ABOUT THE AUTHOR   95

YOUR JOURNEY GUIDE

This is *not* a study guide. It is not a left-brained exercise, all logical, informative, and educational. There are no questions marching neatly across the page, protecting you from getting emotionally involved or trying to manipulate you to get emotionally involved. If that is what you're looking for than there are dozens of those out there, all set up for you to study, memorize, and research.

A relationship with Jesus is personal, making it different for everyone. There are no blueprints for what your relationship with Jesus has to look like. This is a manual of prompts to help you get started, and it is not about thinking, it is about *doing*. Thinking and using our head is much easier than getting actively and emotionally involved. A study guide causes you to think. This will cause you to act. A study guide uses your head, while this gets your heart involved. It is much easier to read about a relationship, discuss it, analyze it, think about it, and write about it, but you won't get to know Jesus doing those things. This manual will walk you step-by-step into a living, breathing relationship with Jesus, your Bridegroom Lover.

It takes time and effort to build a relationship, and you can't cheat because there are no right answers waiting on you to fill in the correct blank. Intimacy with Jesus can't be laid out on paper to be checked off in a hurried few minutes before class starts. Here you can't cram at the last minute, for there is no test. There is no one to judge you or hold you accountable. The depth of your

THE JOURNEY GUIDE

relationship with God is totally up to you. Relationships are personal, so this is not to dictate that you must do these particular things to get to know Him. My point is nothing more than that to get to know Jesus you must spend time with Him. *With Him*, not with other things that we substitute for Him. There is a time for Bible studies, specific prayer times for people's needs, devotions, and worship, but this journey is to get to know Jesus Himself. As Christians we tend to think that the first commandment to love God is performed by the second commandment of loving our neighbor. Those are two different commandments, to love God, and then to love our neighbor. This focus is on loving God.

While this is set up to correspond to one week per chapter, with four days each week, you may want to spend your first week just reading through this initial section before the chapters and days start. There is a lot to absorb and it may take a bit of time. If you find that working through this takes more time than you expected don't worry, there are no rules. This isn't about the goal, it's about the process, and it's better to wait for a good time than to try to work it in when you aren't able to focus and relax.

WHAT TO PACK

You won't need to pack much, a small bag or backpack will do. The things you will use on this journey are more spiritual than physical, and those don't take up much room. Here are a few things you will need:

- A notebook or journal in which to keep notes of what you see and experience. I would suggest that you don't go buy an expensive, leather-bound one, even though some of us have a weak spot towards them, because the reality of it is that when it's that expensive we hesitate to use it in case we mess it up. An inexpensive spiral notebook will lie flat or flip back to stay open to where you're taking notes, so you don't have to find your page again or use a bookmark. Many times Holy Spirit will use your writing to open your eyes to things He wants you to see. By journaling your times with Jesus you also have a record you can read over and over of fresh revelation, encouraging words, and of wonderful times with Jesus.
- A pen that brings pleasure when you write, whether by beauty or the way it flows across the paper.
- A copy of *The Wild Romancer* and of this manual.
- A place where you can be alone for at least fifteen minutes or longer.
- A source of music. You will need background music that helps keep out the noise and distractions but lets you focus on Jesus, and your personal preferences of worship music.

THE JOURNEY GUIDE

- I suggest that you pick up some Post-It flags to mark your place in the book. You can also use them to mark a place you skipped or wanted to refer back to. And whether you use them or not, it's always nice to have a good excuse to buy some Post-Its!
- You will need various other things throughout this journey but I will let you know ahead of time so you can be prepared. When you see the word "PREPARATION" under the day be sure to read it ahead so you can come to your time with Jesus prepared.

BEGINNING THE JOURNEY

This manual is merely to get you started on your journey into intimacy with Jesus. Even if you've read *The Wild Romancer* before, it will help if you read the chapters in it along with the corresponding chapters in this manual, as there is much in the book that will help you on this trip. While the book *The Wild Romancer* is your tourist guide, pointing out the beauty and sights of what you can experience in this place with Jesus, this manual is the itinerary of your own personal trip. *The Wild Romancer* was written to entice people to come and experience this place in relationship, but this manual is about *your* journey.

A LOVE STORY

There is a place of intimacy with Jesus that is so personal, real, and wonderful it is amazing that so few have discovered it. The Bible talks about different kinds of relationships we can have with God, from Master and slave, friends, or Father and child. All are good and all are Biblical, but the closest, most personal relationship that knowing God brings us is that of Bridegroom and bride. We, as Christians, choose our relationship with God. We get to pick how close we get to God, how deep our bond is, and what that relationship looks like. Some prefer the distance in the relationship between servant and master, which requires nothing more than obedience. Some enjoy being friends, while others walk in the warmth of a loving Father. Whatever relationship we have with God while here on earth, our end relationship will be as Jesus' bride.

When Paul is talking about our relationship as the bride of Christ he tells us in Ephesians 5:31 & 32: *For this reason a man will leave his father and mother and be united to his wife, and the two will become one flesh. This is a profound mystery-but I am talking about Christ and the church.* It is in this context of marriage that Paul tells us in I Corinthians 6:17, *But he who unites himself with the Lord is one with Him in spirit.* This passage is referring to now, not just when we get to heaven. In a marriage relationship on earth with another human we unite and become one flesh, and in a marriage relationship on earth with Jesus we unite and become one spirit.

Again, in I Corinthians 6:16-17, Paul puts our relationship with Jesus on an intimate level. *Do you not know that he who unites himself with a prostitute is one with her in body? For it is said, "The two will become one flesh." But he who unites himself with the Lord is one with him in spirit.* This uniting is for now, not once we die.

As Christians, we often start with the relationship we've been modeled, whether it's slave, friend, or child. Many times it's more of a head knowledge, since traditionally we are taught that emotion is suspect. Unless we supernaturally experience God in a particular way, we generally stay with our comfort level of what we've been taught. Traditional church teaches us that God is holy, focusing on hushed services, reverence, and awe. Sunday School teaches us He's a big God who does big things like floods, angelic visitations, and plagues. Vacation Bible School shows us a Father who loves His children. But do we emotionally feel that? Not usually. He's holy. Okay. He's our Dad. Okay. He came to earth as a man so we can relate to him. Okay. We will adamantly declare that we love God, but our emotions rarely move much deeper than that.

This manual will help move your love from your mind to your heart. Until we continually know God experientially, with our heart emotionally involved, we aren't walking in true love.

HE'S DESPERATE FOR YOUR LOVE

This relationship with Jesus is for both men and women. Most men connect their relationships and the love they receive to their performance: at work, home, with kids, parents, etc. However, deep down there is a longing to just be loved and accepted for who they are. Men are problem solvers by nature, and while it is both genetic and environmental that they connect this with love and relationships, they, too, long for a noncompetitive, unearned love and acceptance.

While it is very difficult for men to accept this kind of relationship, they can find an unbelievable freedom when they learn to have this intimacy with Jesus. Jesus is a man's man. He never was and never will be wimpy. He understands hard work and hardship. He understands recreation. He parties. He is strong and firm.

Can men experience intimacy with Jesus and still be "real" men? Ask Peter. Ask John. Ask Martin Luther, or Smith Wigglesworth. Ask my husband Terry. John was "the disciple whom Jesus loved." He had an intimate relationship with Jesus that was different from the other disciples. Yet the book of John was included in the Gospels along with the others. Was he any less of a man because of his close relationship with Jesus? No. What about Adam? He walked in an intimacy with God that was completely natural. Yet Adam also did the work that was his responsibility *and* walked in intimacy with his wife. Yes, it IS possible for men!

THE JOURNEY GUIDE

Most women long to be romanced. We want to be pursued for who we are by a lover who, because of his passionate love for us, will cross any river or mountain to get us. We want to be treasured for who we are, wooed and pursued because we are loved, and romanced by our Handsome Prince. And that's what we get when we fall in love with Jesus as our Bridegroom. He woos us, romances us, and fulfills the longing of our soul for love and beauty, for He Himself is love and beauty. He is gentle, kind, and full of fun. He will press your boundaries, for He wants all of you, not just your masks and pretenses. He will gently draw you further and further into the Romance to end all romances. Moreover, the more you allow Him of yourself, the closer He will come, drawing you into Him, building your trust, and filling you with His love. The more you will make a place for Him, the more He will come to spend time with you, until before you know it He's calling you to come to Him when you least expect it.

Once when I was spending time with Jesus and we were talking about my going with Him leaping over the mountains and skipping over the hills (Song of Songs 2:8), I felt Him say this:

> *First, before we go running together, stop and look at Me. Really look at Me. Look inside Me and see My heart for you. Drop your ideas and notions of what I want and don't want, what I'm ready to judge you for or discipline you for, and just listen to My heart. I'm in love with you. You are My beloved, My spouse, the lover of My soul. Come away with Me, into My inner chambers, into My place of rest, into My private courts and rooms, and let's get to know each other. Drop your masks, your fears, your layers of protective clothing, and show Me the real you. I promise to treat you tenderly, not to wound you or expose you to others who would tear you down. You can trust Me. I promise not to rush you, but I'm anxious for us to be together. I can't wait to walk as one heart, one soul, and one Spirit.*

DESPERATE FOR YOUR LOVE

So, I will encourage you, tease you, woo you, and do anything I can think of to entice you further along with Me. Let's go, I've waited a long time for this. Do you know what it's like to be in love with God? Have you any idea of the places I want to take you and the things I want to show you? I can't wait!

Whether you are a man or a woman, you are leaving home on a journey into intimacy with Jesus. That journey will take you into spiritual realms through Holy Spirit, and into places beyond your imagination. But there is a catch—you have to drop your preconceived ideas, open your heart, and be ready to fly out on an adventure of a lifetime. The wonderful thing is that no matter what your physical life looks like, you can take this journey and it never has to end. The adventure of this journey goes on and on, flowing in and around your physical life. Your destination is to know Jesus, but oh, what adventures you will experience on your way as you fall deeper in love!

WHAT TO EXPECT

This manual is about learning to play with Jesus. Before the fall, Adam and Eve had their work cut out for them maintaining the garden and doing all the work that God had ordained for them, but they also had downtime with God, walking "in the cool of the day" and enjoying His company.

We have a tendency to think that God is all work and no play. We use the excuse "We are supposed to be out saving the lost, we can enjoy Him once we get to heaven," maybe because we feel guilty spending time with Him, or because we do not know how. Maybe we are too busy with life, but most likely it is because we honestly believe it is true. We believe that our relationship with Him is completely service based. In most churches we even consider worship a "service" to Him.

We have been taught that saving the lost is our only goal in life. Yet we forget that loving Jesus passionately is the first commandment and makes it so much easier to go to the world. If all we do is to give out to the world without ever receiving more of Jesus, we will soon burn out and have nothing left to give but flesh.

God wants us to go *with* Him as He performs the business of earth, but in the evening (not literally) He wants us to put it on the shelf and say to Him, "Business is over, now let's play!" Jump in His arms, look in His eyes, laugh with Him, and taste of His goodness. Drink from His river of delights and eat from His table laden with choice food. From this Source comes every answer, every breath, everything you need to sustain you through the business hours. Yet even during times of business you are walking and conversing with Him, and being renewed in His love.

THE JOURNEY GUIDE

Business with Him is never work. It is a small part of the pleasure that is our feast set before us, our Bridegroom Lover, our Jesus.

This manual is about relaxing and getting to know each other, not business, ministry, discipline, or prayer time. It's "walking in the cool of the day" as Adam did, and talking. When writers get "writer's block" they have writing prompts, little writing exercises that start the creative juices flowing. The daily prompts in this manual are to get you started, then let Jesus take your time wherever He wants it to go. If you do something totally unrelated to the suggestion for that day, celebrate! That's wonderful! You can come back to the one you missed another day or skip it altogether. Therefore, I'm going to tell you something that will be very hard for some of you, but listen to why I'm asking this before you get your dander up. During this time with Jesus don't open your Bible unless you specifically hear Him tell you to look something up. In fact, leave your Bible across the room on the shelf or desk where you can't reach it without specifically getting up and going after it. Here's why: many Christians use the Bible as a crutch in their time with God because it's so much easier to read it than actually have to listen and have God speak directly to them. Others don't trust that they can hear God, so they play it safe and only allow Him to speak to them through the Bible. You can read your Bible during your Bible time later.

I'm all for the Bible, but this is not the time to use it. This is not a Bible study. It's much harder to get to know Jesus one-on-one than it is reading about Him, and few people make the effort. We are programmed to have a relationship with the Bible, but Jesus also wants you to know Him. Jesus tells us in John 5:39,40 *You diligently study the Scriptures because you think that by them you possess eternal life. These are the Scriptures that testify about me, yet you refuse to come to me to have life.* Here is an email excerpt I love, written by my friend Maria in Finland:

> *My stepmom said we shouldn't look for experiences but God does give them to us at times. Well, I disagree with this because doesn't God want us to experience Him? It's like getting married to someone and saying "I'm*

WHAT TO EXPECT

happy to have married you. I don't expect to "experience you" but I allow you to let me "experience" you when you choose. But I am not really focusing on experiencing you. I'll stay in this room and read your old emails. Bye!"

Don't do what you're used to doing in your time with God, for example: warfare, Bible reading, intercession, devotions, or prayer lists. If you need music have it low in the background. You should have no crutches to lean on to avoid having to face Jesus.

Now, start listening and watching. It's about doing, not teaching. You can study this, memorize it, and think and dream about a relationship with Jesus, but unless you actually jump in and experience it nothing will happen. A relationship with Jesus won't just happen to you while you go about your normal life, dashing wildly from stress to stress. Lately I've been exceptionally busy and tired and lazy, and Jesus pointed out that when I come to have intimate time with Him I'm wearing my shoes and socks. If I got in bed with my husband to be intimate and romantic but kept my shoes and socks on, my husband would not be impressed, and neither is Jesus. What that means is that when I go to spend time with Him my heart is in a hurry, my mind on what I'm planning to do after that, my head elsewhere. My inward attitude is that I'm going to spend a token amount of time and then I'll jump and run. Emotionally I'm coming to Jesus wearing my shoes and socks. Once He showed me what I was doing I worked to relax, emotionally settling in for a while. So, even if you are limited on your time with Jesus, be sure to prepare your heart and head beforehand to take off your shoes and socks and settle in, not allowing yourself to feel rushed or pressured, as that will totally ruin your time together.

SOME THINGS THAT MIGHT HELP

Your physical destination on this journey isn't all that far, but spiritually you'll be traveling light-years. Don't worry, you were created for this, you're already spiritually programmed for this journey. Physically you'll need little more than a place to be alone, a block of time, and a desire to get to know Jesus. When I first started hanging out with Jesus our family of five lived in a small apartment, where Terry and I shared a bedroom with our four-year-old son. The only place I could be alone was in our tiny laundry room, where I would sit on the washing machine and enjoy Jesus. The children would occasionally wander in with a question but that didn't matter, Holy Spirit isn't fragile and can't be scared away by children. I encouraged them to give me the time alone, but didn't refuse them admittance when they showed up. My special places to be with Jesus have changed over time. Since then I've had a large laundry room, a futon in the garage, my own office, the bed in our bedroom, and at one point a mattress on the floor in the corner of a basement behind a curtain. Your place needs to be somewhere you can be comfortable and where you can relax and close the door, or at least know that others won't walk in on you. The important thing is that, for whatever time you have allowed, you are as alone and as undisturbed as possible.

Sometimes we need to de-clutter our minds and focus on Jesus ahead of time, especially if we have a limited amount of time to spend with Him. It's hard to relax and get to know Him when

THE JOURNEY GUIDE

our minds are going a mile-a-minute. We need to let go of work, problems, stress, and the children, and just mentally relax in a hot tub. Personally, I'm not a hot tub person, I'm more one to sit with my hot tea and look out the window, but I like the feeling the mental image brings of a hot tub, warmth and relaxation, of a time alone to pamper yourself and let go of everything else. This time is not about your prayer list, your needs, your fears and panics, or your agenda. It's about you and Jesus hanging out. So, if possible, start ahead of time with focusing your mind on Jesus and your approaching time together.

Beware of the mind games. If you allow them to they'll quickly destroy anything God says to you. Learn to ignore them. They will tell you that it's not God speaking but your own thoughts, that you're making it up, that you're crazy, and that God would never speak to you that way. Satan doesn't need to work to destroy our relationship with God, our mind is perfectly capable of it all on its own.

Many times we let fear destroy our relationship with God. I once heard a speaker say, *"You get fear and intimidation in your heart and it keeps you out. It's what keeps most people out of the supernatural, the fear that it's not God, the fear of deception, the fear that it's New Age. You have to trust that the ability of a loving Father to keep you is greater than the devil's ability to deceive you."*

If you've honestly tried the prompt and don't feel that you're getting anywhere with it, then just listen to music, worship a bit, dance, lay and soak up His presence, have a conversation, or think of something else to do with Jesus. Often, while listening to music, He'll minister to you and speak, heal broken places in you, or just cover you with His presence. So don't get all hung up on hearing or not hearing, struggling with a blank mind, or what it is supposed to look like. There are no rules. Just hang out, relax, chat, and listen. *But don't do all the talking.* It's easy to get into the talking mode to cover our fear of not hearing anything or to cover how uncomfortable we are being alone with Jesus. Make sure that you give plenty of time to listening.

We often think that to listen we have to blank out our minds, but the trouble with that is that we then can't hear anything

SOME THINGS THAT MIGHT HELP

because we're trying so hard to keep every thought out! You don't have to make your mind a vacuum. Try to keep your thoughts on Jesus and if you find yourself distracted by something else just refocus on Him. Listening is merely training yourself to catch what God says. Imagine what He might be saying, or where he is sitting, or what He is feeling. Imagine His eyes looking at you. Imagine Him laughing, and telling you how much He loves you. That allows your mind to be occupied with Him while keeping your spiritual senses alert.

OTHER HELPFUL HINTS

If my time is limited, one thing that helps me relax and settle in is to set a timer or my cell phone alarm. Sometimes I feel that I've been there ages and wonder what time it is. Maybe my mind is running ahead to what I need or want to do after my time with Jesus, or to the usual stresses of life, making it hard not to keep checking the clock to see if the time is up. Doing that keeps me emotionally distanced, which is not nearly as satisfying as a good visit and keeps an intimate time from happening. Setting an alarm helps my mind let go of the time, even if I end up turning off the alarm and staying longer just because I'm having such a good time.

I'm physically a "doer," sitting still is hard for me. I have too much energy and too many things that I'm wanting to get done, so I have to work at relaxing and settling in for the long haul. Subdued lighting produces a feeling of quietness and rest, so I like to use a lamp or candlelight. I might enjoy a cup of hot tea and possibly cookies, or a treat that's easy to eat from a plate on my lap. Often I'll massage lotion into my hands while we talk, or write our time in my notebook.

My husband occasionally goes for a walk to be with Jesus, but he is doing this less and less because he is learning how to be alone with Jesus and not be physically active. Men go through a more difficult transition from being "doers" to being still with Jesus.

THE JOURNEY GUIDE

I suggest quiet, instrumental background music because it's hard to listen to Jesus and give Him your full attention if you're distracted by wanting to dance, sing, and worship. Those songs are great, but this isn't worship-in-the-throne-room time, it's get-to-know-your-Bridegroom time. Feel free to set apart other times in your day to read your Bible and worship.

Fifteen minutes a day will do if that is all you have (and it beats none all to pieces), but more is preferable, a minimum of thirty minutes is great. I understand that time is a precious commodity, as my brother Dow says, "Life is time-consuming." Because of this I wanted to make this as life-friendly as possible, yet on the other hand, you cannot get to know someone without spending time with them. Therefore, each week I've tried to include both fifteen-minute prompts and longer ones. You can adjust which one you do according to your time needs of that day. I've limited the structured time to four days a week for the same reason, allowing you to have three hectic days without missing any. Ideally, you will have more time than fifteen minutes for each visit, and you will be able to take more days a week to be with Jesus than just the four. Even without a prompt you can put on worship music or come up with your own prompt, or just sit and enjoy being with Jesus. There are often times I'm so tired by the end of the day I just sit and lean my head against Him, enjoying the peace and quiet with Him, even if it's only for five minutes. See? There are no rules.

If you find there are things that you just can't wrap your mind around, then, instead of dropping everything about this relationship, just shelve the troubling parts and move on with the book. Just say, "Jesus, I'm not sure I'm ready for this, so I'm just going to shelve it for now. I want to know You deeper but I'm scared/nervous/uncomfortable with this. Show me Your heart, remove my fear, and take me deeper in You."

Unless it says differently, begin each time by putting on your background music, settling in comfortably, closing your eyes, and relaxing. Take some deep breaths and let go of the stresses and busyness of life. That may take a few minutes, or be easier to do some days over others. Closing your eyes helps you relax and

OTHER HELPFUL HINTS

focus on Jesus. It also makes it easier to see in the spirit. We're so physically oriented that the physical world dominates our senses. Removing some of that physicality helps us discern our spiritual senses.

IS THIS JOURNEY SAFE?

The Bible makes it clear that Jesus loves us enough that He died to get us. It makes it clear that He is our Bridegroom, and that He's madly in love with us as His bride. He knows us and He wants us to know Him. John 10:14 says, *I am the good shepherd; I know my sheep and my sheep know me.* He also tells us in II Timothy 2:19, *The Lord knows those who are his.* That word for *know* is the same word used in the Bible where it talks about how Adam *knew* Eve, in the most intimate sense of the word. That word means much more than to know *about* someone, or to know *who* they are. As I said earlier, Paul himself puts our relationship with Jesus on an intimate level. *Do you not know that he who unites himself with a prostitute is one with her in body? For it is said, "The two will become one flesh." But he who unites himself with the Lord is one with him in spirit.* (I Corinthians 6:16-17) That Jesus *knows* us and we *know* Him is to become one in Spirit, the way a man and woman *know* each other and become one in flesh.

It is Biblical that we hear God speak to us. *When he has brought out all his own, he goes on ahead of them, and his sheep follow him because they know his voice.* (John 10:4)

It is also Biblical for us to know God's presence. *This then is how we know that we belong to the truth, and how we set our hearts at rest in his presence whenever our hearts condemn us.* (I John 3:19-20) Moses experienced God's presence and glory in the Old Testament, and here it tells us (in II Corinthians 3:7-18) that we should be experiencing God's glory and presence even more than Moses did.

> *Now if the ministry that brought death, which was engraved in letters on stone, came with glory, so that the Israelites could not look steadily at the face of Moses because of its glory, fading though it was, will not the ministry of the Spirit be even more glorious?*
>
> *If the ministry that condemns men is glorious, how much more glorious is the ministry that brings righteousness!*
>
> *For what was glorious has no glory now in comparison with the surpassing glory.* (That's us, living in surpassing glory!)
>
> *And if what was fading away came with glory, how much greater is the glory of that which lasts!*
>
> *Therefore, since we have such a hope, we are very bold.*
>
> *We are not like Moses, who would put a veil over his face to keep the Israelites from gazing at it while the radiance was fading away.*
>
> *But their minds were made dull, for to this day the same veil remains when the old covenant is read. It has not been removed, because only in Christ is it taken away.*
>
> *Even to this day when Moses is read, a veil covers their hearts.*
>
> **But whenever anyone turns to the Lord, the veil is taken away.**
>
> **Now the Lord is the Spirit, and where the Spirit of the Lord is, there is freedom.**
>
> *And we, who with unveiled faces all reflect the Lord's glory, are being transformed into his likeness with ever-increasing glory, which comes from the Lord, who is the Spirit.*

Ephesians 3:17-19 tells us we are *supposed* to have spiritual experiences. It is easier to understand this verse if you read it from

IS THIS JOURNEY SAFE?

The Amplified Bible, which takes the translation and expands on its meaning according to the original words used.

> *May you be rooted deep in love and founded securely on love. That you may have the power and be strong to apprehend and grasp with all the saints [God's devoted people, **the experience of that love**] what is the breadth and length and height and depth [of it]; [That you may really come] to know [practically, **through experience for yourselves**] the love of Christ, which far surpasses mere knowledge [**without experience**]; that you may be filled [through all your being] unto all the fullness of God [may have the richest measure of the divine Presence, and become a body wholly filled and flooded with God Himself! (AMP, emphasis mine)*

Lastly, I want to address imagination. We are created in God's image, and with that comes the wonderful gift of imagination. The Bible tells us in several places to not use our imaginations against God, for example, *He hath shewed strength with his arm; he hath scattered the proud in the imagination of their hearts* (Luke 1:51). Here are two more: *Because that, when they knew God, they glorified him not as God, neither were thankful; but became vain in their imaginations, and their foolish heart was darkened* (Romans 1:21), and *Casting down imaginations, and every high thing that exalteth itself against the knowledge of God, and bringing into captivity every thought to the obedience of Christ* (II Corinthians 10:5). These verses show us that our imaginations are of God and we should always use them for his glory.

I love what Luci Swindoll says in her book *You Bring the Confetti – God Brings the Joy.* "Have you ever stopped to consider that every time you listen to music, turn on your television, read a book, go to a movie or a play or watch a comedian perform, every time you view a painting or a sculpture, it is the product of someone's imagination? Every invention and creation began with a 'mental image or concept' of what was not actually present to the senses."

THE JOURNEY GUIDE

Even if something is your imagination, it provides a structure in which to interact with Jesus. Whether Holy Spirit uses it to take you places that are no longer your imagination or not, what matters is the fact that Jesus comes and goes with you there, enjoying the trip with you. Jesus is always with you, but to imagine Him there physically will help you establish a relationship with Him as someone with whom you can relate to as a Friend and Bridegroom. Using your imagination is saying "What if ..." What if Jesus came and we had communion/danced/talked/went on a picnic together. As I tell about in *The Wild Romancer*, my friend Marilyn had a migraine, and as she lay in bed she thought, "What if Jesus came and put His hand on my head and I was healed?" And He did, and she was healed.

We accept Jesus and become a Christian by making a choice, and the depth of our relationship with Jesus is also by our choosing. Because of what the Bible tells us we know that He wants to be one in Spirit with us (see reference above). Holy Spirit convicted me one day on my fear that anything I experienced was "flesh," meaning that it was not really God, just me thinking it was. He asked me, "How can I show you anything when you're so scared it might not be Me that I can't do anything? Your walls are so high I can't get past them. So what if you thought something was Me and it wasn't? It's not the end of the world. So you mistakenly give Me glory for something, is that so bad? I'd much rather you try to learn how to know and recognize Me than to never try in case you fail."

You have to choose to believe that He wants to be with you and that He will manifest His presence to you. You must choose to accept that He is real, that His presence is real, and that you can experience Him. Both your mind and satan will work to talk you out of anything you experience with Jesus, so you must be on your guard against that. When your head whispers, "You just made that up" you say "So what? Leave me alone. This is about Jesus and me, so go away."

The suggestions in this book are a start, a prompt, a beginning. If you feel like you want to do something else, go

IS THIS JOURNEY SAFE?

ahead, mark this place and do it another day, or tack it onto the end of your journey and go a day longer. If there is a time constraint, switch one day with another one that might not take as long. The goal here is to prompt you into enjoying specific time with Jesus, so if He initiates something else run with it. If you start out doing the prompt and it becomes something else, go with the flow, there aren't any rules to this. These are starters, so if you have a larger slot of time then let it be a starting place to take you deeper into other things.

As you work through this book be also looking for Jesus to initiate time together, drawing you to come spend time with Him when *He* wants to be with you. This is a two-way relationship, not only about you wanting to spend time with Jesus but about Him wanting to spend time with you. My heart is to show you what is possible for you and to help you walk into that intimacy. May Jesus pursue you and woo you into such a deep and intimate relationship that you wonder how you ever lived without it. May He take you into such realms of a passionate love for Him that you are lost forever in His arms. I pray that through this book you fall in love with your Wild Romancer.

USE YOUR NOTEBOOK!

I cannot emphasize enough to use your notebook. You will be writing what you experience, how you feel about what you're doing, and your emotions as you go through this journey. You'll be writing conversations with Jesus and thoughts on those conversations. There will be many times later that you want to remember something specific, or refer to something that happened. You need to date every entry, and even if you don't write out full sentences, put down the bones of the experience, even if all you write is "I didn't feel anything today, my head just wasn't there." Be sure to jot down whatever you experience of Jesus, whether it's emotions, things you see or hear in the spirit, know about Him as you're with Him, or just your thoughts as you ramble along in conversation. Even if you feel sure that you're imagining something, write it down.

Often you'll realize later that you weren't imagining it at all. And so what if you *were* imagining it? Write, "I imagined today that I told You a joke and You laughed." I personally prefer to address my talking in my notebook to "You," since what I'm writing is to Him. That makes Him more personal and real to me and it is a way to focus on Him. After all, this time is about you and Him together, and if you're spending your time jotting thoughts separate from Him then this time isn't doing what it is designed to do. It's one thing to write, "I wish I weren't so self-conscious about this, I wonder why I am," and another to write, "Why do You think I'm so self-conscious? I don't want to be. I feel awkward doing this with You." At the end of these twelve weeks you will be looking back over what you've written, putting together in your head what you've experienced and learned.

Don't limit this journal to this particular journey; let it become your spiritual journal by including anything that you spiritually feel or experience. If it's not a particular Journey Guide entry then just date it and write whatever you're experiencing spiritually, whether it's a dream or thought or whether it is experiencing Jesus outside of this prescribed plan. Also, feel free to go back to a particular day and add to it, or continue with that experience later. There are no rules.

Next to actually spending time with Jesus, the most important part of this manual is to WRITE IT DOWN!

Besides your notebook, you may want to keep a notepad with you. (I use small legal pads.) You can jot notes on it during your time with Jesus, and then afterwards clean it up, flesh it out, and write it into your notebook. However, ONLY do this if you will be disciplined enough to write it out in your notebook afterwards.

Read the corresponding chapter from the book, *The Wild Romancer*, at the beginning of each week, *before* your first day alone that week with Jesus. The specific time for each day is not for reading books, it is for being with Jesus, so get your chapter read ahead of time. Some of these prompts take a little preparation, and if there is something to have ready ahead of time it will tell you what you need under the day. So when you finish with the current prompt glance at the next prompt to see if it says PREPARATION. Also, once you start, be sure to read the whole portion first, so that you fully understand what the prompt is asking you to do. If you find that you read a prompt and your heart just isn't in that particular one, or you feel that you don't have the time you want, trade it with another one for that week that better suits your mood or your schedule. Always put the date in your notebook as you do each day's prompt.

EXERCISES

(To be done *before* your first prompt)

EXERCISE 1

In your notebook, all fresh and clean and full of white paper that will soon be full of life-changing notes, write at the top of the first page: HOME (it doesn't matter whether you're physically home or not, we're going to call the beginning of this journey *home*) and **be sure to put the date**. I like including the day of the week with my dates as it makes it easier to go back and look something up, but there are no rules and it is your travel log, not mine.

As you go, either you can choose to write on the back of the previous page or you can choose to start each day with a clean page on the right, depending on your personal hang-ups on wasting paper. I still fight labeling myself as wasteful but I don't like writing over the residue of old ink from the previous page, so I only write on the clean side on the right.

Now, under the label HOME, write what your relationship with God is right now. What is your perception of how you and God relate? Is it Master and slave/servant, Father and child, Friend and friend, or Bridegroom and bride? Is it Stranger and stranger, or maybe it's Big-Far-Away God and little-worm-He-doesn't-care-about? Be honest, and try to be as specific as you can.

THE JOURNEY GUIDE

EXERCISE 2

At the top of the next page write: DESCRIBE JESUS BASED ON YOUR EXPERIENCE. Now do so. No, not what the Bible says about Jesus, not what church has told you about Jesus, and not what you think you know about Jesus. Remember, this isn't a mental study where you memorize Jesus' qualities, nor is it a test to show how spiritual you are, it is a manual to help you physically experience Jesus. Only list things that you have personally experienced, for example, we all know from Sunday School that Jesus loves us, but don't write "He loves me" unless you have experienced *feeling* that love. It doesn't matter how long or short your list is, the purpose is to give you a reference point at the end to see how your experience with Jesus has changed.

It may take a while to get both of these things on paper. Don't feel like you have to get it all down in one sitting. As you go through your day things will come to mind and you can add them later.

CHAPTER ONE

(Read "Chapter 1-The King's Harem" from *The Wild Romancer*)

CHAPTER ONE – DAY 1

This is the beginning of a pursuit of Jesus like you've never known. There will be times that you wonder about the methods in this book, or when this pursuit doesn't look like anything you've ever seen, or when you are asked to get out of your comfort zone. We all have our "box," the parameters of comfort and security we build up over our lifetime. They are based on everything from experience to what we perceive Christianity to be to our upbringing to what we've learned in church. Unfortunately, as long as we cling to our box we can't experience God the way he wants us to, because knowing Jesus isn't about a doctrine or a teaching or learning about Him. It's actually knowing Jesus Himself, and while everything in this study is Biblically based, if we're not familiar with something it can get uncomfortable. It calls for getting out of our safe, comfortable boat and walking on the water with Jesus. Peter hadn't done that before, it was new and scary, but Jesus was out there and he was determined to be where Jesus was, not left behind with the others, playing it safe.

During this journey there may be times when you wonder if you're making things up, or if what you're experiencing is merely your flesh. So what if it is? So what if you're making it up? Holy Spirit sees your desire for a relationship with Jesus and will honor your pursuit of Him. Later, in *The Wild Romancer*, I talk about how when a person is going to build something out of concrete he will first build a form in order to hold the wet concrete. Once the concrete has hardened, the form is removed and the real thing is left. It's the same way with us. We build a form for Holy Spirit to come and fill, and one day you suddenly realize that the form is gone and the real thing is there. You act/live the relationship you want with Jesus, and soon you'll discover that it's more real every day and you need your form less and less. You are showing Jesus that you want Him more than anything else, and He loves to be pursued like that. He loves to find people whose whole heart is after Him, and He delights in coming and entering into that relationship.

Hegai, in the book of Esther, is a picture of Holy Spirit. His job was to prepare the women both physically and emotionally to be with the king, making sure they understood what the king wanted and how to please him. Esther met Hegai in his tasks with an attitude of submission and humility, doing everything in her power to work with him.

Are you ready to let Holy Spirit work on you? We must balance our passion for the King with allowing Holy Spirit to change us to please Him.

Holy Spirit and you are a team. The difference between you and Esther is that your King is already madly in love with you.

Today, if you're ready, pray something similar to my commitment to Holy Spirit:

> *I am the bride and I need You, Holy Spirit, to teach me to know the living God. You are my key. Teach me. It is not only that I have to learn to please the King, but how to get called back into His presence again and again, how to find favor in His eyes, like Esther. I have always wanted to go to the King with no preparation, no training, no beauty, and no knowledge of the art of wooing Him. I want Him to woo me, to come to me, to want to spend every waking moment with me even when I am not prepared nor do I make time for it to happen.*

CHAPTER 1

I can see that I am unprepared for this. I have not taken the time to learn how or listen to my Teacher. I can see that I only wanted the result, the prize without the race, the diploma without the knowledge.

As of tonight, I am entering the School of the Spirit. And I am taking several classes, all taught by the same Teacher, (You Holy Spirit), with occasional appearances by the King. Classes like: How to find favor in the eyes of the King, Pleasing the King 101, Beauty Treatments - 6 months with oil of myrrh - 6 months with sweet spices and perfumes, and How to Act Like a Royal.

School starts now and is always in session. There are no holidays, no breaks, no weekends. On the other hand, to stand before the King prepared is worth every second, every tear, and every moment of lost sleep. The classroom is wherever I am: home, grocery, church, with Christians and non-Christians, with family or strangers. I will try never to miss a class or fail to do my homework. I will try to be attentive, alert, and not to waste time by doing all the talking. I will function in a constant listening-and-acting-on-instructions mode. I will try not to second-guess You. Instead, I will wait on You. I am teachable. Please, oh please teach me.

I give You permission Father, Jesus, and Holy Spirit, to do whatever You want with me, teach me anything, wake me up anytime, stop me, and change me. I am wholly Yours. Change my heart and give me a passion for You. Do whatever You need to do in and with me. I am Yours.

All right, I am ready to begin, now what?

Now enter today's date into your notebook, put on some background music, relax, and listen to Holy Spirit. Imagine that He's there with you and talk to Him today as your Friend and Tutor, instead of as Jesus your Bridegroom. The Trinity is all one God, yet they have distinct personalities and functions. As you go through this journey, instead of one big God in the sky, work on seeing and relating to God as Father, as Son, or as your Friend and

THE JOURNEY GUIDE

Tutor—Holy Spirit. Doing this changes God from being too big "out there" to being more personal and relatable. How do you perceive Holy Spirit? Do you think of Him as God? Do you think of Him at all? Do you feel any emotional involvement with Him? Feel free to write your thoughts in your notebook.

CHAPTER ONE – DAY 2

We have a tendency to have walls when it comes to God. We keep Him at arm's length, hiding behind our masks and facades that we have carefully put in place. We can fool others, but we can't fool God. He sees and knows us inside out. Yet we still try to hide our flaws from Him. He wants the real you, not the person you want Him to think you are. We're usually afraid He'll judge us, or lecture, or condemn, or tell us we have to straighten up, but He won't. Jesus doesn't condemn, He forgives. Holy Spirit convicts, it's satan that condemns us. We're often much harder on ourselves than Jesus is.

Your assignment today is again with Holy Spirit, letting Him see the real you. Yep. And the quicker you do it the easier it is. Until we let Holy Spirit assess what He needs to do to make us ready for the King, He can't change anything. Let Him begin the myrrh bath and the soaking and scraping. He's gentle and kind, and He loves you. He won't hurt you, He makes it better. He gently rubs away the hurts and wounds, the pain and heartaches, the embarrassments and shame.

Tell Him that you don't want any secrets, that He is allowed to strip everything away and wash you clean. As He brings something to light show it to Him, accept His balm, and let it sooth and heal. Become aware of your attempts to cover and make excuses for your failings and flaws. A big excuse we love to use is that such-and-such is just our personality. Listen to Holy Spirit and be honest with Him. For example, some things that He's pointed out to me in the past are that I'm judgmental, critical, too analytical, and I want everything perfect. In other words, "lighten up." I have a tendency to emotionally put up a protective shield to

CHAPTER 1

keep from getting hurt, and He wants to walk with me every step of the way and deal with my hurts Himself. How are you doing things your own way? What armor are you wearing that He wants you to remove? Again, write down what He shows you.

CHAPTER ONE – DAY 3

Today I want to change your perspective. We have a tendency to imagine/view/expect Jesus to be in the sky, so our talking, praying, and body language is usually either upwards or with bowed head acknowledging His being "out" there. It's time to change that perspective.

You will occasionally find yourself falling back into the old perspective of God-in-the-sky, but keep at it and it'll get easier.

Today I want you to see Jesus sitting here with you. Imagine Him as if He were physically sitting here in the room with you. It helps this viewpoint if you actually have an empty chair or place to sit by you, but it's not necessary. In the spirit He can be sitting by you no matter where you're sitting.

Therefore, if I'm sitting on my bed then I imagine Him sitting on the bed by me. When I had my office with the overstuffed chair, I imagined a chair across from me where He sat, even though physically there wasn't one. This is easier to do if you close your eyes. Jesus is spiritually there with you, so imagine Him in human form. This won't happen overnight, and you'll catch yourself relating to Him "up there," but no matter where you are or what you are doing, work at seeing Jesus physically with you. It will make Him seem much more personal.

Now, you have a block of time. You're sitting here alone, expectantly. You have your notebook and pen within reach. *Now what, you wonder. This feels awkward. I'm excited and scared. I haven't the foggiest idea of what to do. I'm assuming this manual is going to tell me and not leave me hanging.*

Close your eyes. Take a couple of deep breaths, and say something to Jesus. Don't worry about being spiritual, profound, or prayerful. This is chitchat time. I usually start out saying,

"Hey" or "Hey Jesus" or "Hey, it's me, I'm back." We laugh together and are off from there. Just start a conversation, whatever comes to mind. Talk a bit but don't forget to stop and listen. If, after a few minutes, you begin to feel lost or blank, just begin to write what you think Jesus might be saying.

For example, I might start a conversation like this: "I've had my shower and am all ready for bed. It's a strange thought that You're always up, You never sleep. I love sleeping. You slept when you were man, but You didn't have a wonderful mattresses, pillow, and electric blanket. No king-sized bed for You, just outdoors on the hard ground with Your cloak to cover You. So You probably don't miss it like You would if You'd had my bed. You don't know what You're missing, it's wonderful! I know You don't sleep, but I'll bet You goof off and relax, it's Your nature to laugh and be joyful. So did all those years sleeping on the ground make You want to camp or turn You against camping? I'm not a camper myself."

Need help? Tell Jesus what the best part of your day today was/is going to be and what the worst part was/might be. Ask Him how He could have been/be in the worst part with you.

Chapter One – Day 4

Can you just choose to have a passion for Jesus, just say, "I'm now going to be passionate about Jesus" and then you are? No. Holy Spirit has to quicken that passion in you. Jack Deere, author of *Passion for Jesus*, tells how he wanted a passion for Jesus but didn't know how to make that happen. So he began to pray every day that he would have a passion for Jesus. After a few months, he realized that he now had a passion for Jesus, but it had happened gradually, it wasn't something that had hit him suddenly. So *ask*, not once but repeatedly.

As you work through this journey you are showing Jesus that you're serious about loving Him, and He won't disappoint you. In your time today ask Jesus for a passion for Him. Tell Him how much you love Him, that you're pursuing Him and won't give up,

CHAPTER 1

and how much you want to know Him deeper. Tell Him your heart, your dreams, your hurts. And listen. Feel Him as He puts His arms around you and holds you. Feel His heart as He loves on you. Listen as He sings love songs over you. Just be still and sense His presence. Start experiencing what it feels like to be alone with Jesus.

CHAPTER TWO

(Read "Chapter 2 — The Key That Unlocks the King's Bedchamber" from *The Wild Romancer*)

CHAPTER TWO – DAY 1

PREPARATION: A piece of paper (any color you want that will show markings), pen, markers, crayons, whatever you need to draw a picture.

I encourage you to write your feelings, fears, and how it's going as you go through these prompts, so you can later look back and see how your relationship is changing. I find that many times as I'm writing I begin to hear Jesus and Holy Spirit speaking to me through writing out my thoughts. No, not that He "takes over" my pen, but that as I write I begin to understand things that surprise me and make me realize that He's speaking to me even when I'm not aware of it.

Today you're going to draw a picture for Jesus. Don't panic, it won't be a work of art, you don't have to show anyone else, and you don't need anything other than paper and pen. You don't have to be artsy or creative. Take your paper (even white printer paper is fine), and draw a representation of you (a stick figure is fine), but make it look like you in some form, whether it's hair, a plaid shirt, or your favorite shoes. Now write or draw something on it to Jesus. You can decorate it as much as you want or as little as you want, there are no rules. Just tell Jesus something on the

THE JOURNEY GUIDE

picture that is from your heart to His. Now show it to Him and tell Him about it. He'll enjoy putting it on His fridge.

Write in your notebook what emotions you experienced doing this.

CHAPTER TWO – DAY 2

Imagine that you and Jesus are sitting near each other. Imagine that you are interviewing Him about His life on earth. Have your notebook ready, and ask Him what pleasures he enjoyed during His life as a man. What brought Him pleasure? Think about it a few minutes, and don't get all Biblical and say faith. What I want is for you to see Him as a person, with likes and dislikes. Think about what it was like as a man in those days, walking all over the hills and towns, and teaching. What are some things that might have brought Him pleasure? Nothing is too small or too simple to mention. As you think, take time to listen, see if He speaks anything into your mind about it. Often what He says will surprise you. Things you would never expect Him to say. Then start writing your thoughts. Write them as if you were interviewing Jesus. What would He say? There are no right or wrong answers, just let go and stop struggling with lofty thoughts. If you get that done quickly, move on to some other questions. What were some of the hassles or frustrations He experienced? As you think of things, write them. It's very likely that by the time you're finished you will be surprised at the things you wrote. Often Holy Spirit will prompt you and give you ideas and insights.

CHAPTER TWO – DAY 3

PREPARATION OPTIONAL: the sound of waves on a beach, whether with music or not (internet is a good source)

CHAPTER 2

With background music on and notebook ready, imagine that you and Jesus are walking along a beach. You don't have to talk, just comment on things if you want, no pressure to keep a conversation going. Simply walk, or stand and watch the waves. Imagine that you can hear the waves, are they lapping or crashing? Can you feel the spray? The wind? Are you barefoot or wearing shoes? If you're wearing shoes take them off. Feel the sand under your feet as it shifts and packs to support your weight. Is it dry sand or wet? How do you feel about getting wet sand on your feet? I found when I did this that I was uncomfortable having sandy feet, I like my shoes and socks on. It stretched me to relax and not care about getting sandy and wet. Does the grass grow down to the edge of the sand, or sea oats, or flowers? Or are you just on a huge beach? Look for shells, do you find a good one? Work to keep Jesus in the picture with you, for example, what's He doing as you walk? What emotions do you perceive Him having?

CHAPTER TWO – DAY 4

In your notebook, under today's date, think of something, anything, and write a word or phrase, whatever comes to mind (it probably won't be spiritual, don't expect it to). Now take that and just start writing, but write it as if you're telling Jesus. What does it make you think of? What emotional connections do you have with that word or phrase? Just write off the top of your head, letting thoughts stream straight through you. That way your left brain will get out of the way and let your emotions and creativity ramble on.

I tried it, and got "cookies 'n cream." So here's what I wrote:

Okay, it can refer to a complexion—hey! That reminds me of the new song I heard this morning. For some reason when she sang "I've seen His kindness" it sounded like "I've seen His countenance." I liked what I heard better, I want to have seen Your countenance. But I just realized that a complexion is peaches 'n cream. What's cookies 'n cream? A snack? Good things? That's

THE JOURNEY GUIDE

you Jesus—good! Actually, now that I think about it, it's a flavor of ice cream—AHA! You like ice cream, you told me so! Is that what kind you like? I'll have to get us some. Ben & Jerry's—like that kind? I'll get us some Ben & Jerry's Cookies 'n Cream ice cream. I'm glad you didn't pick Cookie Dough. :)

Doing this kind of exercise isn't to give you deep spiritual insight, it's to help you become comfortable hanging out with Jesus. It's to help you relax and stop trying to be so religious. This is have-fun-getting-to-know-Jesus time. Lighten up and laugh.

CHAPTER THREE

(Read "Chapter 3 — Spiritual Reality" from *The Wild Romancer*)

CHAPTER THREE – DAY 1

PREPARATION OPTIONAL: Your ocean waves music again.

There is a difference in God's *manifest* presence and His *omnipresence*. God is omnipresent, meaning that He is everywhere at once. There is nowhere we can go where He isn't with us.
Psalms 139:7-12 tells us:

> *Where can I go from your Spirit? Where can I flee from your presence?*
> *If I go up to the heavens, you are there; if I make my bed in the depths, you are there.*
> *If I rise on the wings of the dawn, if I settle on the far side of the sea, even there your hand will guide me, your right hand will hold me fast.*
> *If I say, "Surely the darkness will hide me and the light become night around me," even the darkness will not be dark to you; the night will shine like the day, for darkness is as light to you.*

God's manifest presence is where He allows us physically to experience His presence. He *wants* us to know Him, to know His love and His joy in us, and the more we make a place for Him in our lives the more we experience His manifest presence, and learn to recognize it.

Today you're at the beach again. Tell Jesus that you want to experience Him both physically and spiritually. His heart is towards us and He *wants* us to know Him. It delights Him for us to ask. Therefore, instead of the usual background music, put on some quiet worship music, lie down on the floor, and "soak" in God's presence. (If you have a CD with the sound of waves on it play it.)

Now imagine that you're lying on the beach and a wave washes up around you. That wave is God's presence and love, washing away your fears, hang-ups, and doubts. Feel the water on your skin; can you breathe under the water? If imagining that your face is underwater makes you uncomfortable then just lie at the edge of the waves and let them wash over you. Feel your hair as it floats away from your head as God's presence covers you, and just let Jesus love on you. Feel Him healing old wounds and hurts. Imagine Him washing away all the dirt the world has put on you, from music in stores you have no control over to fussy words you've said or heard to the stresses in your world. All of those issues at work – let the waves wash them away. The waves keep washing over you, more and more, until you're lying in the ocean of His presence as it swirls around you and lifts you into His arms. Immerse yourself in Him, feel His peace flowing through you.

CHAPTER THREE – DAY 2

God *wants* us to experience Him. It is not His intention to have us live our lives as if He only exists when we read about Him in His book. Being Jesus' bride isn't merely living with head knowledge of Him until we die; He wants a love relationship with His bride *now*! That's why we have Holy Spirit in us, who draws us to Jesus.

In the same way that you have physical senses, you also have spiritual senses. Jesus often talked about our spiritual senses. For example, in Matthew 13 He says, *They hardly hear with their ears, and they have closed their eyes ... But blessed are your eyes because they see, and your ears because they hear.* Again, in Mark 8 He says, *Do you have eyes but fail to see, and ears but fail to hear?* He wasn't talking about the people's physical eyes or ears. God is Spirit. We cannot experience Him to the fullest if we don't use our spiritual senses. Throughout this guide we work on helping you practice using your spiritual senses.

Today think about how easily you experience God. Have you ever realized that you *could* experience God? If possible, remember a time or times when you experienced God, for example, felt His presence, knew He was with you in a vivid way, or when you felt especially close to Him. Maybe a time when He took away your fear and gave you peace or when He specifically spoke to you. Make a note of these times in your notebook, enough that you can later read it and remember the experience. How well do you feel like you hear God? Your spiritual ears enable you to hear Holy Spirit's guidance, hear your Daddy God speaking loving words to you, and to hear Jesus wooing your heart.

CHAPTER THREE – DAY 3

The spiritual realm, through Holy Spirit, is an incredible place, and it is where we get our resources for living the Christian life. God has provided supernatural resources for us to help us through this journey on earth, but we have to take them out of our backpack and use them, just carrying them with us doesn't help us. Resources like, for example, our ability to have an intimate relationship with Jesus and then to move in His love and compassion to the world around us. Resources of revelation, the ability to move in signs & wonders, and financial discernment. Unless we learn to walk in the supernatural, spiritual realm through Holy Spirit, we cannot experience God's presence, or all that He has for us.

THE JOURNEY GUIDE

Today I want you to think of something positive you have experienced in the last few days using each of your physical senses, (touching, tasting, smelling, hearing, and seeing). Think back over the last week, have you eaten anything that tasted especially wonderful or seen something that was so beautiful it took your breath away? List the five senses and then beside each sense write what it was that comes to mind for each one. Now list the five senses again, but this time think about those senses in a *spiritual* way. In front of each sense tell a way you could spiritually experience that sense.

CHAPTER THREE – DAY 4

PREPARATION: Do this preparation a full day before your next time alone with Jesus, whether it's the morning before you get with Him that night, or whether it's yesterday morning if you meet with Him in the morning. In other words, part of this prompt happens throughout your day, to be talked about in your time alone with Jesus. Take five scraps of paper, then choose five of the following colors and write them on the papers: navy, turquoise, orange, silver, lime green, burgundy, purple, and peach. Fold each paper, shake them together, and then draw one. Every time you see that color today stop and listen to see if Holy Spirit has something to tell you. Even if you feel you don't hear anything pause to look for Jesus, to feel Him, to sense His presence. Jot notes of what you feel or think.

The things you are learning and experiencing here should become a lifestyle, not just something limited to a tiny portion of your day. Work on fostering an awareness of Jesus' presence in your life all the time, and on noticing Holy Spirit's guidance and help. Listening is so important, probably the single most

CHAPTER 3

important aspect of the Christian life. If you can't listen you can't hear, and unless you can hear God you cannot have a relationship with Him. Do you listen to others when they're talking, or are you so busy planning what you're going to say that you miss what they're saying? Do you *really* hear what they're saying, or is your mind elsewhere? If you don't listen to the people around you, chances are that you don't really listen to God either, whether you perceive that you do or not. Listening is a habit that becomes a lifestyle, and it takes time and patience to become a good listener. It is making a choice to stop what you're thinking and doing and just listen, even when you might not think you're hearing anything. Are you serious about hearing Jesus and Holy Spirit, or are you going to give up after a few minutes?

Today in your time with Jesus read over the things that you felt that He was saying to you as you saw your color. Did you hear anything? The things Holy Spirit says to you may not seem monumental. Don't worry about it. Again, these are merely suggestions to get you to focus on Jesus. There are no rules. If you didn't hear anything today then ask Him what He is saying to you now. If you have a hard time getting anywhere, just start writing what you think He could be saying and listen as you write what comes to mind.

CHAPTER FOUR

(Read "Chapter 4 – Developing Your Spiritual Senses" from *The Wild Romancer*)

CHAPTER FOUR – DAY 1

The first line of this chapter in *The Wild Romancer* is so true I want to repeat it. *To live a life without using our spiritual senses is to live the Christian life without experiencing God.* You cannot experience a relationship with Jesus unless you are not only emotionally involved but you can experience *His* emotional involvement. In the book "Song of Songs" the Beloved and the Lover are both emotional, they each experience the love of the other. Tommy Tenney says, "I am afraid that we have satiated our hunger for Him by reading old love letters from Him to the churches in the Epistles of the New Testament. These are good, holy, and necessary, but we never have intimacy with Him. We have stifled our hunger for His presence by doing things for Him."

Have you ever experienced something and then later explained it away? We love to make excuses for why something is not God. Wouldn't God be surprised to find someone that had a hard time believing that anything *wasn't* Him?

Think of some things in the last few days that had a positive emotional impact on you. What are some things you think about that cause negative emotions? How can relating to Jesus as your Bridegroom and spending time with Him emotionally affect you? Emotions from your time with Jesus will bring joy throughout your day, as you not only remember your time together but also as you become more and more aware of His continual presence.

CHAPTER FOUR – DAY 2

In this chapter I talk about the Malaysian woman who, in a dream, was taken by Jesus into different rooms, and in each room she was struck by how few people were in the room. Each time she asked Jesus about it He replied with the same answer, "No one ever asks to come in here."

Think of a room you would be interested in visiting with Jesus. The Malaysian woman went into the musical instrument room. I've been in the Dance Studio, His Treasure Room, and the Sword Room. My husband Terry has been in the Worship Room. Once you've decided, ask Jesus to take you into that room and show you around. Close your eyes and imagine walking up to the door, opening it, and seeing inside. Just start imagining what you might see, and let Holy Spirit show you things. You may not feel like you're seeing anything that isn't your imagination, and that's fine, there are no rules.

When Terry went into the worship room he didn't see music or instruments. He saw only arms and faces. He asked Jesus about it and He said that this room was full of what people offered up in worship. "This is all they ever give Me."

I've learned that many times when you think that you've just imagined it all, when you go back and write down what you saw you realize that there were aspects that Holy Spirit showed you that at the time you didn't realize was Him.

Even if it's your imagination it provides a structure in which to interact with Jesus. Holy Spirit may use it to take you places that aren't your imagination or He may not, but it doesn't matter as much as the fact that Jesus comes and goes with you there, enjoying the trip with you. Whatever you do in your imagination, always imagine Jesus there with you. He *is* always there with you, and to imagine Him there physically will help you establish a relationship with Him as a person instead of the invisible One.

CHAPTER 4

CHAPTER FOUR – DAY 3

Do you operate more from your right brain or your left brain? If you are organized, meticulous, structured, detail-oriented, logical, and critical you are left-brained. If you tend to be creative, artistic, feeling-oriented, imaginative, and see the big picture, you are more right-brained. Left-brainers have a harder time experiencing God's manifest presence as they are quick to logically explain everything away, and aren't used to allowing themselves to experience things emotionally. I had an epiphany one day as I hung out with Jesus.

> *I just realized something. I'm over here in the cabin and I've been looking up stuff in the Bible studying the Greek. I can't find any music that I can tolerate. I've walked the circle of the rug thinking and feeling as if I'm getting nowhere and this is boring. I'm wondering how to get somewhere spiritually, so far I've wondered around lost. But I just realized something. I've been using my mind, my logical thoughts, my "mental conceptions," as Daniel 4:5 calls it.* I saw a dream which made me afraid, and the thoughts (mental conceptions) upon my bed and the visions of my head troubled me.
>
> *I try to go places in the Spirit through my mind and thoughts, but how is that possible? I can figure things out, get revelations, meditate, and chew on stuff, but I can't go anywhere in the Spirit doing that because my mind is in control, keeping my mental facilities in the left brain. And the left brain will never go places spiritually. That's why left-brained people have so much trouble in the emotional area. We must learn to leave the thinking, left-brain, logical side of mental conceptions and move over to the right brain, where the spiritual senses are.*
>
> *The spiritual senses are right brain, because to see Jesus, smell His fragrance, feel Him, taste Him, and hear*

THE JOURNEY GUIDE

His voice you have to be on the right side of your brain, shutting down your analyzing side.

So what I'm saying is that instead of standing and thinking and trying for something spiritual to happen I need to move over to the right side of my brain. There I imagine things, using my spiritual senses. I imagine smelling Him, traveling with Him, touching Him, hearing Him, eating with Him, anything in the Spirit. I do things with Him. Instead of thinking about doing things I imagine doing them. Instead of thinking about walking through the woods with Him I close my eyes and start walking. Instead of trying to think of a good revelation to chew on I actually do something with Jesus. Practice, practice, practice. I can do that anywhere anytime. I need to take my own advice. Notice I'm sitting here writing and doing the mental thing instead of going over there and doing it. Okay, I'm off.

Pick one of the choices below or one of your own, and imagine participating in it with Jesus. Let your imagination run wild as you experience the sounds, sights, smells, tastes, and feeling of being in your imagination with Jesus. He is bigger than your imagination. You have asked Him to help you and He will. You have to believe that God's ability to keep you is greater than satan's ability to deceive you. Many times Holy Spirit will use it to take you into the spiritual realm so that it's no longer all your imagination. You know that has happened when things occur that you wouldn't normally have imagined in that particular way. Often you don't realize that it wasn't all your imagination until afterwards when you're writing about it in your notebook. So don't worry about it and enjoy the adventure!

Imagine:

- Meeting Jesus at a restaurant and eating with Him.
- Going hiking with Jesus.

CHAPTER 4

- That you and Jesus have climbed a large tree and are both sitting on a limb talking and looking out over the countryside. What do you see?
- Playing golf, paddling a canoe, or going fishing with Him.
- Picking a specific place that you've always wanted to see, and then going there with Jesus. It doesn't matter if the real place looks like that or not, this is your imagination.

CHAPTER FOUR – DAY 4

Write down at least four different smells that you associate with a memory, good or bad. What emotion do you experience as you relive that memory? What smells do you find pleasure in? Many people have experienced a wonderful supernatural fragrance in their time with Jesus. Ask Him what smells He enjoyed when He walked in skin. Which ones did He not like? If you don't feel like you get anything then guess some answers and write them down.

CHAPTER FIVE

(Read "Chapter 5—Summoned By the King" from *The Wild Romancer*)

CHAPTER FIVE – DAY 1

We walk out our relationship as bride in many different aspects, for example, the bride in intercession, warfare, the five-fold ministries, and worship. Of all the aspects of the bride though, the bride in intimacy with Jesus is where we get our supernatural love and compassion to minister to the world. As He ministered to the world through His intimacy with the Father so we can only effectively minister as He did out of our intimacy with Him.

Who tugs at your heart? When you're out or when you hear about something, which stories grab you? It can be anyone from the persecuted Christians in China to babies, from single mothers to the elderly. It might be orphans or prostitutes. I recently heard of a ministry that was started for people who work third shift. No one is unimportant when it comes to Jesus' heart.

I've discovered I have a particular burden for people who struggle with weight gain. My heart understands how hard it is. I've found myself in tears just seeing an overweight person at Wal-Mart. I've once dreamed I was praying for an overweight person to be healed, and woke crying. Recently I discovered another group that holds my heart, and that is people who have to drive a piece of junk. There have been periods during our married life where we struggled to have a roadworthy car. There was a time early on when we drove a pick-up truck that didn't have reverse or first gear. Another time it was a Volkswagen Rabbit that could only be clutch-started. We know firsthand how expensive and painful car repairs can be, so when I see a car held together with coat hangers and duct-tape my heart bleeds for them, and I begin to pray that God will provide them with a new car.

In your time today think about a particular group of people for whom God has given you a burden, and tell Jesus about it. Ask Him for ideas of ways to make a difference in those people's lives. Tell Him that you want more of Him and His love and compassion to take to the world, and you know that it has to come supernaturally from Him. If no particular group has caught your heart yet then ask Jesus to help you notice who that might be.

CHAPTER FIVE – DAY 2

Start your background music, close your eyes, take some deep breaths, and relax. Imagine Jesus standing in the middle of a field. Walk out into the field to meet Him. Now, ask Him to show you a place that is special to Him. Where would He like to go? Now just start walking with Him and see where you go. If you're stumped just keep walking a bit. Where would you imagine Jesus especially enjoying? Start imagining that place and Him showing you around. Maybe instead of going somewhere special with Jesus He wants to do something else. Jesus once asked my husband Terry to play pool with Him. Terry told Him that He'd have to limit Himself or Terry wouldn't have a chance of winning. They had a great time together. Let go of your critical analytical brain and your restrictions on what He would say or do and have some fun with Jesus.

CHAPTER FIVE – DAY 3

PREPARATION: a notepad to jot notes on

CHAPTER 5

besides your notebook

I've had people question me about how knowing Jesus as our Bridegroom affects our relationship with our spouse. They ask questions like "Wouldn't your husband be jealous?" and "What part does your husband play when Jesus is your Bridegroom?"

One night a friend dreamed that Jesus came and proposed to her, and brought her flowers. After the dream, He continued to woo her into a relationship with Him as her Bridegroom. She became so happy, so full of Him that when her husband would get home from work he would want to know why she was so happy. She told me that with Jesus meeting her needs she doesn't have to depend on her husband, or be disappointed in him. Now when her husband remembers to be romantic and send flowers or a card she loves it and appreciates it, and now, instead of wondering why it took him so long to get around to doing anything special she can just enjoy that he thought about her. She's overflowing with Jesus' love and attention so that she is happy and ready to give her husband attention when he gets home. Men, the same thing works in reverse.

Often, when people marry, they both have deep needs that they unconsciously try to fulfill from their spouse, so the marriage becomes a struggle as each try to get their needs met. When Jesus begins to meet their needs they no longer have to pull from their spouse, they have the life and love to give to their mate that comes with a healthy marriage.

With Jesus meeting your needs for love and romance, you no longer have to depend on your mate to meet needs that he/she often isn't capable of meeting. You're free to love and enjoy what he/she can give you without demanding it. You can accept them for who they are. Jesus heals your neediness, putting your marriage back onto a more stable track and filling your love tank so that it can overflow to your spouse.

Only you know your spouse, so only you can determine how much of the details to tell them. Some will just need to know the basics, that you're enjoying time with Jesus and this time is changing who you are, and because of that you are finding that you love your spouse more. Use wisdom in telling your spouse about your time with Jesus. However, you will find that the relationship will flow out over the rest of your family in a wonderful way. Your spouse will begin to enjoy the benefits of you loving Jesus and not resent the time you spend with Him.

What would be a fun date that you would love to share with your husband or wife? It could be a candlelight dinner, fixing your favorite dessert, flowers, a gift, candy, watching the ballgame together, or eating out. Maybe it's just some time together walking and talking, receiving compliments and words of appreciation, or getting a back rub.

Sit and imagine sharing that date with Jesus. Close your eyes and see Him romancing you, loving on you, and doing something special with you.

Using your notepad write a love poem (it doesn't have to rhyme or be long) from Jesus to you. Once you have it the way you want it, copy it into your notebook. Then read it aloud as if Jesus is reading it to you.

CHAPTER FIVE – DAY 4

PREPERATION: Look through a magazine or search online and find a picture of scenery or an activity that pushes your button. Tear it out or print it so that you have a copy. NOTE: if finding the right picture takes more than an afternoon then skip this prompt and move on to the next. Then, once you've found the right picture, come back and do this one.

Sit back and relax. Pick up your picture you have ready and study it a minute. Pick out the spot where, if you were with Jesus, you would be standing or sitting. Now close your eyes and imagine being in that spot with Jesus. In the movie *Mary Poppins* Burt, Mary Poppins, and the two children jumped into the chalk picture on the sidewalk. They had all sorts of adventures inside

CHAPTER 5

the picture. Look at it that way. Are you walking or standing still? Is there a place in the picture that looks interesting, that you want to walk over and explore more closely? A cabin? Behind the rocks? In that grove of trees? Wading in the water? Where would you put yourself and Jesus into the activity? Are you doing the same thing or enjoying competing with each other? Spend time with Jesus in the picture, enjoying each other and talking, or just enjoy being quiet together. Let Holy Spirit lead what happens. Now write about the experience, no matter how simple or short, or unimportant you might think it is.

CHAPTER SIX

(Read "Chapter 6 — Seeing Jesus" from *The Wild Romancer*)

CHAPTER SIX – DAY 1

Ruth Heflin says in her book *GLORY* that revelation always begins with the Lord.

> *The revelation may be simple at first as you begin to see Him. Some see only His feet. Some see only His hand. Some see His face ... 'The knowledge of the glory of God' comes from the 'face of Jesus Christ.' Therefore, we must be those who see His face ... This is not just an added privilege for a select group of people. It is given to every one of us to have eyes that are anointed to see.*

The first thing to realize is that you won't see Him physically, you'll see Him with your spiritual eyes. That means that you can see Him whether your physical eyes are open or closed. Until you're used to seeing Him it will be more of an impression than seeing His whole form clearly. You may not be able to tell specifically what He is wearing, how his hair is parted, or what His shoes look like, but you will know whether He's smiling or laughing, whether He's standing or sitting, and you will know that He's there and what He is doing. You may only see a part of Him, or you may sense His whole body. Jesus cares about our heart, knowing our background and our needs in Him. That means that while we can tell stories of our experiences, that

THE JOURNEY GUIDE

doesn't mean that there is only one way to see Jesus, or that He will look the same to everyone. Some see Him in robes while others see Him in jeans and a tee shirt. I usually see Him in a robe but one day He came in His wedding clothes. Here's an experience our daughter had (the grammatical construction is from a quickly written email).

> *saw Him tonight at 6:08 (college service i attend) we were worshipping, and it's huge, like 10 piece band, 1,600 college students. i was all in the zone and worshipping and everything and i look on stage and there is jesus, and he's dressed in his "sunday school clothes" white robe and everything, barefoot and all that jazz. well, he's up there and he's directing the band and us singing and the angels exactly like a black gospel choir director! very big movements and everything. soooo funny and cool. cracked me up. very whoopi goldberg in sister act. lol.*

However you see Jesus does not mean that everyone sees Him the same way. We can all enjoy sharing stories and experiences, but in no way does your experience, or mine, set the model. In *The Wild Romancer*, chapter five, I tell about my experience in the bedchamber with Jesus. My niece Jennifer has had a similar experience, and we sat one night and compared bedchambers. There were aspects of our experience that were amazingly similar (one end of the room open to the outside), and other aspects that were different (in her experience there was a small table with food that she ate). That doesn't take away from either experience, it just shows me how much Jesus cares and how personal the relationship is. When it is just you and Jesus the experience is specific to you. The church speaks of a personal savior. They have no idea how personal He really is.

As you relax and close your eyes, imagine some aspect of Jesus. Not all of Him, just one part, maybe His hand, or His robe, His eyes or smile. One day I was hanging out with Jesus and I found that His hands fascinated me, so I spent a long time holding

CHAPTER 6

and studying them. Another time it was the back of His shoulders and head. Start out with imagining how you think one of His features might look.

CHAPTER SIX – DAY 2

Stop worrying about whether it's your imagination or not. Either it is your imagination and Jesus is living it with you or it is Holy Spirit taking you places in the spiritual realm. Today you're going to have some fun with Jesus. Sit back, relax, and imagine you and Jesus are going to dive for treasure. Pick where you're going to dive, is it in the ocean or a lake? I could give lots of suggestions but I want you to come up with the details. So out of your imagination find a body of water deep enough to dive in. Get creative. Do you need or want diving gear? Do you jump in from a boat or the side of the body of water? Or a plane? Imagine all the details of diving using your five senses, the feel of the water, its temperature, the sounds, the sights. Can you see clearly or is it murky? Explore under the water with Jesus, swimming around, looking for treasure. What surprises you about the dive, and what do you find? What are your impressions, what emotions do you experience?

Now, as every day, write out what you did, what happened, what you said to each other. I often take notes during my experiences with Jesus so I can remember specific things He says and the order of things that happen. It doesn't spoil it as I can then close my eyes and be right back in it. The act of writing it down often helps you see that it was more than your imagination, and it adds to your collection of things to go back and reread later. David tells us in Psalm 143:5, *I remember the days of long ago; I meditate on all your works and consider what your hands have done.* That word for "meditate" means to relive or remember something repeatedly.

CHAPTER SIX – DAY 3

THE JOURNEY GUIDE

Today I'm going to tell you something it took me a while to learn. Maybe not always, but in my experience, the physical can't touch the spiritual, so don't try. When you're experiencing something in the spiritual realm using your spiritual senses, it can seem so real that you're afraid to move in case you spoil it. Or it may be so real that you wonder if you reached out and touched Jesus would you be able to feel Him? When I was in the bedchamber with Jesus I was afraid to touch Him in case everything just burst and disappeared like a bubble, so I just stood where I was and looked. I realized later that I could have gone over to Him and danced and enjoyed Him but only by doing so in the spirit. When I was eating with Jesus He was so real I wanted to physically reach over and touch Him but I was afraid to. Now I know that I would have physically felt nothing, but if I'd reached over in the spirit, in other words, seen myself in my "mind/spiritual eyes" reaching out, I would have felt Him in the spirit.

You interact in the spiritual realm, not in the physical. You may be physically interacting with Jesus as in dancing or eating together, but in the physical if you reach out you won't feel anything. What you do is to reach out or touch in the spiritual. Physically sit still, but in the spirit reach out, hug, touch, and interact. If you choose to dance with Jesus in the spirit instead of physically, you'll physically be still while spiritually dancing, and it's a lot of fun, especially since there are no limits and you can do anything: twist, twirl, and dance in slow motion without ever running into furniture or being limited by walls. You're dancing "in your head," yet in reality you're dancing with Jesus in the spiritual realm.

Terry interacts with Jesus spiritually in running together, swimming together, and once they wrestled. Terry also dances with Him. The main thing is not what you do with Him but that you interact with Him.

Most of the time when I hang out with Jesus I just sit in my overstuffed chair with a lamp on or candles burning. I like low light since glaring lights are distracting to me, and unfriendly. I

CHAPTER 6

put on my earphones with my MP3 player because that way I can listen to the music as loud as I want.

However, there are times when I physically act out, as much as possible, what I'm doing with Jesus. If it's a picnic I sit on the floor, or on a blanket as if I were physically having a picnic. If I'm dancing I put on worship music and physically dance, often dancing with Jesus even though I can only see Him spiritually, so that while in the physical my hands look like they're against air I can see in the spirit that they're with Jesus' hands. When I eat with Jesus I really eat. That makes it easier to imagine being there, which is the easiest way to enter into the spiritual realm, until you're experienced at it. Start by using your imagination and then let Holy Spirit take you there.

Today I want you physically to act out doing something with Jesus. If you're sitting on the beach then sit on the floor as if you were on the sand. If you're dancing, dance in the position you would be if you were really dancing with Him, with your hands as if they are holding or against His. Or lie down on the floor and spiritually be on the grass on a hilltop looking at the stars together. Go outside and jog around the block with Him. Think of something and physically act it out. This is easier with your eyes closed, so you can "see" better. I have a hard time imagining or seeing in the spiritual realm as easily with my eyes open.

CHAPTER SIX – DAY 4

PREPARATION OPTIONAL: A deck of playing cards

Today, play Rock/ Paper/ Scissors with Jesus, at least four or five times. The key is to play quickly without letting your mind interfere. You play physically and He'll play spiritually. You should see His hand with your spiritual eyes as He plays. Get a real deck of cards and play war with Him. Talk and interact with Him as you play. Now talk with Him about the games you both played as children. Which were your favorites? Why?

CHAPTER SEVEN

(Read "Chapter 7 – Incense Trees and Ice Cream" from *The Wild Romancer*)

CHAPTER SEVEN – DAY 1

PREPARATION: Relaxing worship music that you enjoy.

Put on your worship music, today we're going to soak. It's hard to be still and soak to rollicking music that keeps your foot tapping and your innards bugging, so don't try to soak to fast music. Lie down on the floor, it doesn't matter where, but if you don't have carpet then put down a rug or blanket, (you won't be able to relax and enjoy yourself if you're on the cold, hard floor). You can even have a cushion under your head if you want. Now, don't do anything. What is going to happen is that you're going to relax and soak up God's presence. Try to keep your mind from going everywhere, work to just lie there and let the music just happen to you. Don't sing along. DON'T DO ANYTHING.

You're allowing God to soak you in His peace and rest, to soak you in His presence, and as you do He begins to change you. He breaks off things, He heals, He comforts. He laughs and enjoys you. You may find yourself crying, or laughing hysterically, but most of the time you won't realize what He is specifically doing, just let Holy Spirit move in you. There is no limit to how long this can go on, the longer the better, and if you end up falling asleep, so what? You're resting in Jesus.

CHAPTER SEVEN – DAY 2

The purpose of these exercises is to get you used to being with Jesus. They are to get you used to expecting to feel His presence, *looking* for Him, and making a place in your life for Him to come be with you. You need to be comfortable with Jesus, to know His presence, to feel Him calling you to come spend time with Him. Until you become familiar with His presence and with experiencing Him with your spiritual senses, you will miss Him, feel awkward, or be scared of experiencing Him.

Was there a secret place you had as a child? Or a favorite book with a secret place? I loved books with secret places. As I mentioned in *The Wild Romancer*, one was in a hollow tree and one on a secret island. As a child I would pretend I was an orphan and had run away from the orphanage. I would imagine the wonderful cave I was hiding in while an imagined storm raged outside the cave entrance. Think back to a secret place you enjoyed as a child, whether real or imagined. Take Jesus there and show Him around. Tell Him why you enjoyed that place, what emotions are attached to it.

CHAPTER SEVEN – DAY 3

Sit and think for a few minutes about yourself as Jesus' garden, His place of rest and escape. Men, if you find the whole garden thing too sissy then use the image of a "yard." Wherever it says "garden" insert the word "yard." Ask yourself the questions from this chapter.

- Is He welcome in my garden?
- Can He spend time in my garden without feeling rushed or hurried?
- Is my fruit sweet to His taste?
- Is He pleased with my landscaping?
- Is it available when He wants it?

CHAPTER 7

- Is it a place of rest and peace?
- Is it loving and serving or controlling?
- Do I have a joyful garden?
- Does He feel special in it, having my full attention?
- Is it enclosed, for Him only?
- Is it fragrant and lovely? Well tended and inviting?
- Can He converse, or do I do all the talking?
- Do I keep my garden so perfect that He cannot relax and enjoy it? (He might mess up the scenery by picking flowers or eating fruit. Or He might leave footprints on my perfectly manicured grass.)
- Are honeycomb, honey, and milk there for Him?
- Do I have choice fruits and all the finest spices available?
- Do I have wine for Him to drink and lilies or nuts for Him to gather?
- Is there thanksgiving and the sound of singing?
- Does it bring Him pleasure?
- And most important of all, is my love there for Him?

He adores you. He wants desperately to be with you. Imagine your ideal garden. What would be in it? What style would it be, English with high brick walls, intimate with small paths, flowers or trees, manicured or wild? Golf course manicured or mainly trees and shrubs? Now take Jesus and show it to Him, walking and talking together and just enjoying each other.

CHAPTER SEVEN – DAY 4

Write down 3 things God could be saying to you but you're sure that He isn't, not things that are against the Bible, but things in your daily life. For example, He might be telling me "Take that trip you've always wanted to Paris." Or, "You're giving all you have away, you need to keep some of yourself for you." How about "You're holding your relationships too closely" or "It's time

THE JOURNEY GUIDE

to let go." Now, why do you think that He's not telling you that? If He were telling you to do it would fear stop you? If you make any decisions in your life that are based on fear than you're not living in the freedom that God has for you. How are you limiting God in your life through your fear? How can you change to move more freely in His destiny for you?

CHAPTER EIGHT

(Read "Chapter 8 — Pictures of Men" from *The Wild Romancer*)

CHAPTER EIGHT – DAY 1

Today I want you to spend time with Holy Spirit. By now you should be getting comfortable with Jesus, but it's very important that you also get used to being with Holy Spirit. Being with Holy Spirit involves using your spiritual ears as you focus on listening. You should foster walking in a constant listening mode throughout your days and nights, always being attuned to Holy Spirit. He is your Friend, your Helper, and your Tutor.

Get in your usual comfortable place and spend a few minutes just relaxing and letting go of the day. You may want your background music or you may just want silence (if that is possible in your life right now). I love the silence, and many times find it easier to hear without music playing, but you have to have a quiet place for that to work.

Now, just listen. Take your notebook and pen and write things you hear. Talk. Ask questions. Tell Holy Spirit that you're sorry you don't know Him better but you want to. Ask Him to help you become familiar with His voice. If you can't get going and your mind is blank, just start writing your questions and your thoughts. If you think you know what Holy Spirit might be saying than write it as if you were hearing Him. You'll be surprised at how He will speak to you as you write.

THE JOURNEY GUIDE

Here is something I wrote one day as we hung out.

Who are You Holy Spirit?
I can't figure You out.
Some days You're so clear,
Other days so elusive.
How do I describe You?
You are variety, color.
Gentle, with a thread of steel
You are comfort that satisfies
And fellowship that sparkles with life.
You live in me,
but You're like catching a rainbow in a butterfly net.

What are You really like?
Do You love me?
Have I mentioned that I can't figure You out?

I encourage you to date and write about all your daily experiences, either as you're experiencing them by jotting notes or afterwards, when you can write more detailed. They will be invaluable later as you look back on your journey into intimacy, and give you wonderful things to go back and read later, things that will "take" you into Jesus' presence.

CHAPTER EIGHT – DAY 2

Make up three "Bible verses" that you wish were included in the Bible. No, you're not "adding or taking away" from the Bible, you're just thinking of things that you wish God had said in the Bible. Now read them to Jesus and tell Him why you wish they were in there. Now read them again, but this time, as you read them, hear Jesus reading them to you. Next let Jesus tell you a "verse" He'd like to hear from *you* to Him. Write it down and read it back to Him.

Chapter 8

CHAPTER EIGHT – DAY 3

(To be read in the morning.)

Today is not about a particular time with God, it's an exercise to help you realize that your relationship extends to all day every day; your time alone is just the foundation on which you live your life. Today I want you to spend as much as possible being aware of Holy Spirit. Listen throughout today for at least three things that He is saying to you, through any medium: kids, TV, billboards, anything that catches your eye or ear. Write everything down, even if it doesn't make sense at the time. Most Christians are programmed for God to speak to them only through their Bible, so today put it aside and listen for Him to speak to you other ways. One obvious way He speaks is when something catches your attention. Stop and think about what it was, and ask Him what He is saying to you. It won't necessarily be something huge, it may be nothing more than how much He loves you, or that He's pleased with you.

One day I took my mother out shopping and it seemed that everywhere we went there were cement trucks. One in front of me, another time one was beside us, or turning in front of us. I don't normally notice cement trucks, but this day they seemed everywhere. I finally thought to myself, "Good grief! What is it with cement trucks?" That was my cue. "Okay Holy Spirit, what are you trying to say?" And He spoke great encouragement to me about how, in our ministry and business, Terry and I have built the forms and He has the cement is on its way to fill them.

Keep your spiritual senses honed as you move though your day, and as you go jot notes about what you experience, then later flesh it out in your notebook.

CHAPTER EIGHT – DAY 4

Today, come up with three things in your life that have the potential of distracting you away from time with God, and tell

THE JOURNEY GUIDE

Holy Spirit about it. He doesn't want to take all your fun away, but we need to practice moderation or we begin to make idols of things we love, turning to them so much that we no longer have time with Jesus.

I have found that writing is one of my distractions. Even if I'm writing *about* God, if it consumes all my time, then my writing has become an idol. Sleep is another one for me. I will use the excuse that I'm sleepy, even if I've had enough sleep and fifteen minutes won't make any difference.

Terry's distraction used to be playing golf. Then he started physically playing golf with Jesus, turning the distraction into more time together. Once when Terry hit a fairway shot to the green he missed the green entirely. Frustrated, he heard Jesus say "Drop another ball and hit it again." He did, coming closer but still missing the green. Jesus again told him to hit another ball.

"What's going on," Terry asked.

"It's called grace," Jesus told him.

What is there in your life that distracts you or is your excuse for not having intimate time with Jesus?

CHAPTER NINE

(Read "Chapter 9 — The Richest of Fare" from *The Wild Romancer*)

CHAPTER NINE – DAY 1

PREPARATION: Have a treat prepared ahead of time to share with Jesus, for example, tea or coffee, cookies, or fruit.

Settle in and enjoy your treat. Tell Jesus about how good it is and why it brings you pleasure. Imagine, in the spirit, that He is eating it with you, experiencing it for the first time. What does He think? Just hang out and talk as you eat together. Savor the flavor.

He created you with your five physical senses so you can experience pleasure. Today the pleasure is through your taste buds.

CHAPTER NINE – DAY 2

Imagine being a three-year-old and sitting on Jesus' lap, playing and letting Him love on you.

Destined for You.
Before time began we were
destined for each other
You've always known me

THE JOURNEY GUIDE

You played with me as a child
Held me in Your lap
Fed me dainty sweets and delicacies
dripping with honey.
We laughed, and I had no idea
I belonged to You
I only knew You loved me.
You were security, You were fun.
As I grew older You were always there,
my strength, my friend
Gently wooing tenderly but I still didn't know.
I didn't know I belonged to You
I thought we were just friends forever.

Now, when I hurt – I run to You.
When I need a Friend I know where to look
When I'm lonely, tired, and frustrated
I only want You.
And finally, I see now what I'm destined for,
What I've been trained for all my life.
I was promised to You from the beginning
But You've wooed and loved me,
until all I want is to belong to You completely.
To fulfill my destiny as I stand at Your side
and become Your bride.
So that's why You were always around –
I belonged to You!
You could have claimed me anytime
but You wanted me to love You, to want You
so You've waited patiently for me
to fall in love.

Well, I have!
I love You, I need You, I want You,
I can't live without You!
Don't wait any longer – come and get me!
And by the way, thanks.

CHAPTER 9

Name the top three most delicious dishes of food you've ever eaten. Ones that you relish the taste of, that stood out as paradise on the palate. Tell Him about them: what they were, what was in them, and where you experienced them. What made them emotionally connected to the memory for you? Now let Him tell you what He enjoys eating.

CHAPTER NINE – DAY 3

PREPARATION: To take place eating out in a restaurant or at a coffee shop

Eat out if possible, preferably alone but if someone is with you it won't matter. Without them knowing what you are doing, imagine Jesus eating with you. Either pick out an empty chair at your table or imagine a chair pulled up to the corner by you. As you eat, feel Jesus' presence there at the table while you talk to Him in your spirit, making Him a part of your meal.

If you can't eat out today then do the same thing wherever you're eating, or save this one for when you do eat out.

The goal here is to physically experience eating with Jesus. To be aware of His presence and listen to Him, carry on a conversation, even if it has to be around socializing with another human being. Just know He is there, laugh, tell jokes, and enjoy Him.

CHAPTER NINE – DAY 4

PREPARATION: A special breakfast treat to eat.

Today you're going to eat breakfast with Jesus, just the two of you. Prepare your coffee, cappuccino, hot tea, or whatever you consider a treat to drink. Have something to eat that isn't messy so you can eat off a plate in your lap. In addition, you want something that doesn't matter if it gets cold, as you're going to relax and not rush through breakfast. It may be a cinnamon roll, Danish, or fancy cookies. Now, enjoy your breakfast with Jesus.

For example, here's an excerpt from my journal:

I had a fun time at breakfast this morning. As I bit down in a big fat grape I said, "You must always be thinking 'Oh wow, I created this!'" I picked up another grape. "Look at this awesome grape! How cool is that?"

He gave me a look with a funny grin and said with a definite lack of enthusiasm, "Yeah, cool grape."

And I realized that he's had grapes from a world that wasn't fallen, and he's had grapes from heaven, which makes my little grocery store grape pretty sad. And we cracked up, the look on his face as he had looked at my grape was hilarious!

"One of these days I'll show you a REAL grape," he told me.

"And I'm holding you to that," I said.

I've laughed over that all morning. He's such a hoot!

Talk about your expectations for the day. Ask Him to help you stay focused on Him no matter what the day brings. Think about things that you can do to bring your focus back to Him throughout your day.

CHAPTER TEN

(Read "Chapter 10 – On Sandaled Feet" from *The Wild Romancer*)

CHAPTER TEN – DAY 1

PREPARATION: Music to dance to.

You may be a dancer, or you may not be a dancer, but either way, man or woman, dance is spiritually very important. Ruth Heflin says in her book *GLORY* that "there is great anointing in dancing before the Lord, even if all you can do is tap your toes." Just dance. Dance in worship and dance across the nations, claiming them for God. Dance your feelings, your hopes and dreams, and your emotions. Ruth Heflin also tells us, "The Lord showed me that if we wanted to bring in the Ark of God (II Samuel 6: 12-16) we would have to dance too. ... You need that anointing to flow through you every day. Dancing brings that anointing."

I love dancing in worship, as it is a physical way to give God every part of me. Music is powerful in the spiritual realm. Music matters a lot to God, or He wouldn't have had Lucifer hold such a great musical position. Our bodies were created to be moved by music, both emotionally and physically.

I love dancing alone, just worshipping, my body and heart reaching upwards to a wonderful God who loves me. And I love dancing with Jesus, right there with me, hand to hand. Sometimes I'm just imagining that He's there dancing with me, other times

He comes and dances with me and I can see Him with my spiritual eyes.

As a Jewish man, Jesus would have danced often and with other men. He would have danced at weddings and festivals. Terry has learned to dance with Jesus, and as he opened up to the idea it became a deeply impacting experience.

Today, dance. Fast, slow, graceful or bumbling, just dance. It doesn't have to be designated Christian worship music. It can be whatever music sets your feet tapping. However, as you dance, imagine that Jesus is there dancing with you. You can dance together or you may both do your own thing. It doesn't matter, as long as the two of you dance.

Chapter Ten – Day 2

Today, get in your usual, comfortable spot, relaxed and with your dance music playing. Close your eyes, and dance in the spirit. Notice how free you are and how well you are dancing. The sky is the limit; you have all the room you need. Dance to any music you enjoy. Just relax and have fun, and notice how much Jesus enjoys Himself.

Chapter Ten – Day 3

PREPARATION: A prop to dance with.

Put on your dance music but today pick out a prop to use as you dance. Here are some suggestions:

- a scarf or piece of cloth (I've even used a small red tablecloth I bought at a yard sale.)
- a bridal veil
- a rain stick or musical instrument
- a full skirt, dance shoes, flowing dress, hat, etc.
- a sword or staff

CHAPTER 10

- a ribbon streamer (a child's or make your own from sewing long pieces of flimsy cloth together into a long ribbon attached to a small dowel rod)
- a dance flag or banner
- a favorite hat, or make a cape and dance with it

CHAPTER TEN – DAY 4

Preparation: candles (Men, this is a girly one, get creative and come up with your own idea here.)

Okay, this one needs to be in the evening, when you're relaxed and ready to settle down at the end of your day. I know, you're probably tired and just thinking of bed, but this won't take long. Find some candles and dance by candlelight. You will want slow, soft music, so you that you can close your eyes and focus on dancing. If you must, just dance in one spot swaying and moving your arms. Dance with Jesus together or each do your own thing. The first time I did this it took a while to find candles since I'm not much of a candle person, so after scrounging around I came up with seven candles, mostly Christmas ones. By the time I finished, my little office smelled pretty strongly of pine and cinnamon, but the candles create a whole different atmosphere. Enjoy!

CHAPTER ELEVEN

(Read "Chapter 11 – The Wild Romancer" from *The Wild Romancer*)

CHAPTER ELEVEN – DAY 1

God wants lovers, not slaves. This guide is to help you change your perception from a God who is ready to judge you to a God who loves you deeply and wants to know you intimately, and for you to know Him. He is in a good mood and is not mad at you.

Suppose that Jesus lived in a house and had a room that He used as His own, for example, an office or a library. Use your spiritual eyes and look around Jesus' room. You want to discover things about Him by studying His room. What décor would He use? What would His special things be? Close your eyes, and imagine a room. Is it large, cozy, friendly, and masculine? Make yourself look around and see things. This is a harder exercise, so force yourself to "see." You might see treasures, resources, books, maps, pens, trophies, or awards. Again, I don't want to make too many suggestions as I want this to be *your* imagination, not mine. What type of room are you in? Write and describe what you see in as much detail as you can. Don't worry if you're imagining it or not. Make yourself see as many details as you can.

THE JOURNEY GUIDE

CHAPTER ELEVEN – DAY 2

Today think over your times with Jesus, or about dreams you've had from God. What are some physical items that you can get to remind you of those times? For example, after a fearful day God spoke to me in a dream about the flower known as Heart's Ease. He was using that to tell me that He was in control and not to worry, so I now have a cup and saucer with pictures of Heart's Ease on it. When I look at them I am reminded of God's peace and care. God has spoken to Terry and me that our destiny involves Trinidad, so I have a dollar bill from Trinidad on my desk where I can see it. Terry received a word once that he has wineskins of New Wine hanging on him that cause others to laugh and bring joy, so I bought him a small figure of "Happy," the Disney dwarf from *Snow White*. He also has a wineskin hanging in his office. I had a dream about a red semi-truck that spoke to me about our son's life, so I have a Matchbox one like the one in my dream sitting where it will remind me of what God is doing in our son's life. Because I love to walk on the beach with Jesus, I have some small shells lying on my desk that I picked up recently on our trip to Florida. Now every time I see those shells I am reminded of how much fun Jesus is and of our times together.

So, think over your experiences with Jesus. When there is something concrete get a replica and keep it to remind you of what God has spoken to you, and of your times with Jesus.

CHAPTER ELEVEN – DAY 3

Have your notebook by you as you sit, relax, and close your eyes. Allow yourself to let go of everything and just focus on you and Jesus. Take some deep breaths, and think about how these last few months of hanging out with Jesus have changed your relationship with Him. How are you different? Is it easier to relate to Him? Do you feel His love more? Are you more relaxed in His presence? Have you seen Him? Write a "thought" in your notebook, expressing to Him how He makes you feel. Later go back and rewrite it into some prose or a story that you can keep handy to reread when you need to be reminded of how much He loves you. For example, here's one I wrote:

> *You're my peace.*
> *You're my pleasure*
> *You're my joy.*
>
> *You're my island of escape*
> *My private lush garden*
> *You're my Prince, who holds*
> *me close and loves my cares away.*
>
> *Mmm – I don't want to leave.*

CHAPTER ELEVEN – DAY 4

> **PREPARATION: Have a copy of a poem, prose, or short story that you enjoy, maybe something you loved as a child. Not a spiritual, Christian something, that's too easy, choose something that you just get pleasure out of reading.**

Today read your poem, prose, or short story to Jesus. This is about sharing who you are. What sparks something in you? Is it the way it rolls off your tongue or the rhythms as you read it? Maybe it is the ideas it conveys. I love the poem "The Owl and the Pussycat" by Edward Lear, and Robert Lewis Stevenson's "Escape At Bedtime." Make a note in your notebook of what you read so you can remember it.

CHAPTER TWELVE

(Read "Chapter 12 — I Take You, My Beloved..." from *The Wild Romancer*)

CHAPTER TWELVE – DAY 1

After a few minutes of quietly soaking up Jesus' presence ask Him speak to you or show you something encouraging about someone you know. Just listen until you feel like He's given you something, write it down, and then when you have a chance, call them and tell what God spoke to your heart about them. Stop panicking. Lower your expectations of what I'm saying about nine levels. It doesn't have to be profound or deeply spiritual. It could be as simple as, "Hey, I was praying/in my quiet time/hanging out with Jesus, and I felt that He wanted me to tell you that ...." The key here is twofold. One is to listen. Listening is an art that's hard enough to do with other humans, but it is especially hard to cultivate the habit with God. We have a hard enough time stopping our busy lives and stilling our minds long enough to truly listen, but we must also learn to push past that and actually hear Holy Spirit speak to us. The other key to this exercise is for the pleasure of blessing someone, encouraging them that God cares about them enough to personally speak to you about them. It's amazing how much it encourages someone for God to speak something personal into his or her life.

CHAPTER TWELVE – DAY 2

Are you ready for some fun? Today you're going to cuddle. Yep, just cuddle. Get your timer ready, as sometimes this can start out awkward, and you'll need more time for this one. Get comfortable, close your eyes, relax, and focus on Jesus. Imagine that He's sitting by you and you can just lean up against Him. You're just going to talk a while. Tell Him about your hopes and dreams, your disappointments, and what you want out of a relationship with Him. Tell Him how hungry you are for His love, and how much you want to supernaturally experience His presence. Just enjoy each other, and let Him love on you.

CHAPTER TWELVE – DAY 3

All right, we've reached Part 2 of describing Jesus. Get your notebook and once again write across the top of the page: DESCRIBE JESUS BASED ON YOUR EXPERIENCE, and date it. Now just sit back and think about your time with Jesus over these last few months. Go over in your mind different experiences you've had with Him, and think about what you learned about Him during this time together. List every aspect of Jesus you can think of.

Now, turn back to the beginning of your notebook and read what you wrote in your first description. Is your list any longer? How has your perception of Him changed? I suggest that you type up this second list and print it out, then add it to your collection of things that take you into His presence when you read them, because just reading over this list will bring a smile to your face as you remember each thing you have experienced.

CHAPTER 12

CHAPTER TWELVE – DAY 4

Today think back over your life remembering at least one place with special memories. A place you hold in your heart that belongs to you. Now take Jesus there and let Him experience it with you. Tell Him why you love it, what made it special, and what sounds, sights, and smells were there. What made the emotional connection for you?

Here are a few of my special places:

- Standing on a beach in southern Thailand during the rainy season, under an overcast sky with the roaring of the huge black waves pounding the shore. It was both frightening and exhilarating.
- Walking inside a glacier in Alaska through a tunnel of blue ice.
- A place near the college I attended where we could climb to the top of a rock hill and see for miles over the treetops.
- Staying in a small chalet at the foot of the Swiss Alps as a teenager, where I climbed out my window, up a bank, and into a field of wildflowers.

CONTINUING THE JOURNEY

FEED YOUR LOVE

Love is an emotion, an action, a routine, a choice, and a state of being. It can be exhilarating, the most painful burden we've ever borne, or both at the same time. It is an entity in itself; it has a power and life of its own. Real love is God.

However—love as an emotion needs to be fed in order to keep it fresh and emotionally close. Physically we have everything from holidays set aside for love, to gifts and cards, to physical contact. We have any and all of our physical senses to use in expressing and receiving love.

However, giving and receiving love with Jesus is a completely different matter. What does that look like and how do we do it? After working your way through this book you should have a clue.

However, love must be fed. Without feeding love our emotions cool down, withdraw. Love becomes a memory, and our hearts grow distant. Reliving old memories is wonderful but we must also continue with new ones. Therefore, we must learn how to feed our love. Our testimony of Jesus is not what He did for us years ago when we first believed, it is the fun and communion we've had with Him in the last few hours.

As humans we have holidays to remind us of love—Valentine's Day, Mother's and Father's Day, and birthdays. Invent some spiritual holidays to celebrate your love with Jesus, and then put them on our calendar. There is no limit to spiritual holidays. What are some things you can do to celebrate your Jesus-Day?

Ephesians tells us that God gives spiritual gifts to us. What are some spiritual gifts you can give Jesus?

We can't have the physical contact as in a human relationship, but we have our spiritual senses — how can you use them to feed your love?

Pursue Jesus, listen to Holy Spirit, and EXPECT!

ABOUT THE AUTHOR

Brenda Cobb Murphy and her husband Terry live in Bluegrass Kentucky with their three children. Their oldest son and his wife have recently bestowed the title "Grandparents" on them, causing no end of excitement and joy.

Though both of them come from a strong Southern Baptist background (Brenda was born and grew up as a missionary's daughter in Thailand), Terry and Brenda met at a Charismatic fellowship in college, where Terry was one of the leaders. There, the manifest presence of God showed up in numerous supernatural ways and started them off on a journey with Him that has been an incredible adventure. Over the years they have been involved in worship, conference speaking, prophetic dance and pageantry, and teaching. They have since gotten involved in God's current revival, which has changed their lives and shown them that God can be very physical, supernatural, and awesome.

Terry and Brenda currently travel and teach Kings Boot Camp, enjoying the thrill of watching Holy Spirit move in mighty ways in people's lives, teaching them to walk naturally supernatural.

To learn more about Brenda's ministry visit:

www.brendacobbmurphy.com

CPSIA information can be obtained at www.ICGtesting.com
Printed in the USA
LVOW12s1018090714

393562LV00001B/61/P